JUST BECAUSE IM YOUNG

Emily Michniak
Taylor Krissa

Copyright © 2021 Emily Michniak

All rights reserved

The characters and events portrayed in this book are fictitious. Any similarity to real persons, living or dead, is coincidental and not intended by the author.

No part of this book may be reproduced, or stored in a retrieval system, or transmitted in any form or by any means, electronic, mechanical, photocopying, recording, or otherwise, without express written permission of the publisher.

ISBN: 9798773248613

Cover design by: Emily Michniak
Library of Congress Control Number: 2018675309
Printed in the United States of America

To all who are told they are too young

CONTENTS

Title Page
Copyright
Dedication
just because im young
you're not too young to have heartache   2

you're not too young to have sorrow   59
you're not too young to fall in love   86
you're not too young to feel true happiness   103
    112
About The Author   114

JUST BECAUSE IM YOUNG

TAYLOR KRISSA

They said I'm too young to feel a true heartache
They said I'm too young to even know what sorrow is
They said I'm too young to know what love is
They said I'm too young to know what true happiness is
Just because I'm young I wrote a book to prove them wrong

YOU'RE NOT TOO YOUNG TO HAVE HEARTACHE

The promise ring was supposed to turn into a wedding ring
The valentines day flowers were to be a wedding bouquet
You promised forever.
Now the ring is tarnished and flowers wilted
I guess forever isn't as long as I thought

I am so madly inlove with you
   -liar

You promised sunrises and sunsets
You promised to never leave and yet you left
You promised picnics and starry nights
You promised till death we part
But you ended it that night

I want the kind of love in fairytales
The one where you know how it'll end
I want the love at first sight
The raging passion
And the happily ever after
Why did we end in disaster?

You taught me what love is
Now all is compared to you
There is not one who could out-do
How am I supposed to forget you?

We aren't going to work out
We both must always be right
And that won't end well

Sometimes it's not love. Its just infatuation. You're an addict. You keep going back to them for the high. For how they used to make you feel. It's a trap... stop falling into it.

The trauma in his life messed him up
You thought you could fix him
Not realizing it is yourself you need to fix first
Two negatives do not make a positive

My mind keeps telling me to leave
That the high you leave me with is not worth the low
But my heart is telling me you are the only thing that will ever bring me happiness

I knew when we met you would change my life
I knew you would leave a mark
I knew you would hurt me
I knew I loved you more than you loved me
   -I really hate it when I'm right

You broke me as if you were breaking in new shoes

If I could go back in time I would make sure we never met

How nice it must feel to be the sun
Always being the center of attention
The moon infatuated with its light
and a devoted follower always right behind
I wish I could attract you as much as the sun attracts the moon

She thought she was special
Until she found out she was just your toy.
Something you picked up off the playground
It was something new so of course It had to be yours.

You loved me so fiercely that I burned
I even gave you the matches to burn me with
I didn't care if it hurt
The love was worth the pain
We started a wildfire
But it ended in ashes

Sometimes I think I can forget you
But I'm reminded by the memories
That you will never leave

My stepdad always liked you
The way you shook his hand and how you got along
He liked how bright my face got when I spoke about you
He started asking when you are coming over again
How do I tell him you broke my heart?

Why am I begging you to forgive me when it is you who hurt me

I still see you everywhere

You were the only one I ever wanted to impress

TAYLOR KRISSA

I gave you everything
Any little piece I could offer you
And it still wasnt enough to make you stay

The punches you threw at me were covered up with make up and flowers.
Forgotten by taking me out to dinner and buying me gifts.
Thrown away by movie nights and a ring.
You thought I would forget the abuse if you said I love you

I crumble at the thought of you, while you have already forgotten my name

Why can't you be him

To you I was just a phase
To me you were supposed to last a lifetime

I miss the feeling of being a part of your family
They had no responsibility of me
But took care of me anyway

You built me into your life
But I wanted to build a life with you
I wasn't even your concern
But you were my only priority

Please talk to me
I can feel you drifting away
And there is nothing I can do to fix it
Our relationship is not a never ending waterfall
It is a little pond
And I am the only one filling it

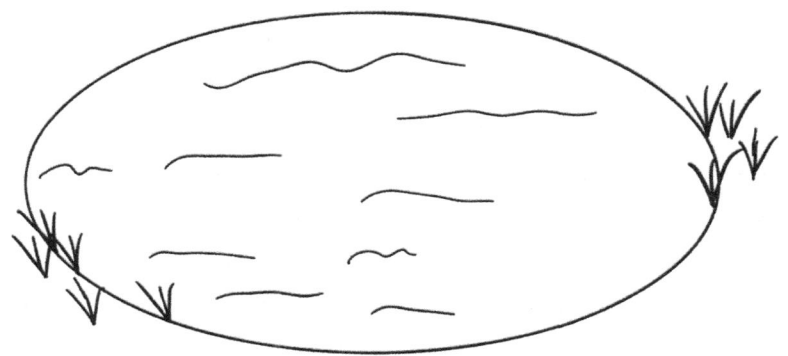

I don't know who I was before you
I still don't know who I am after you
I do know I'm not happy without you

You filled my heart with laughter and love
Now it's like a empty glove
I miss your laugh
I miss your hugs
I miss you and all your love

I say I'm fine
But on the inside it's like a knife stabbing me over and over
I just can't get over the scars you left me

He said I was beautiful
He said I gave him butterflies
He said I was the one
He said we would be together for life
Why do men always lie

You left
And you took everything with you
But you forgot one thing
Me
You forgot me
How could you forget me

How could you erase me from your mind
You told me I meant the world to you
You even wanted me back again
But now we're just a memory

It's not you leaving that hurt the most
It's my mind creating scenarios as if you were still apart of my life
That tears me apart

Forever is what you promised.

It was all the promises that lead me to believe you would never leave
It was all the little gestures that meant the world to me but meant nothing to you
You don't notice anything about me
Why does loving you have to be so painful

My heart broke when I woke up and forgot you weren't mine

You used me over and over again like how your dad used the word sorry to your mom

I think about you so often I forgot I'm not supposed to

When I was young I thought love was supposed to be easy
But it turned out to be
 heartache
 pain and
 disappointment

Why did you say you loved me when all you did was treat me like a burden?

When you said you loved me I thought you meant me not my body.

I lay in the field of flowers
I know I should apreciate the heat of the sun, the fresh air, or the colors of the flowers

But all I wanted you by my side

When we met you got me to let down my walls
Now that you left my walls are back up

The more you used the word sorry the less I want to believe it

The laughs came with screaming
The hugging came with fighting
The I love you's came with tears

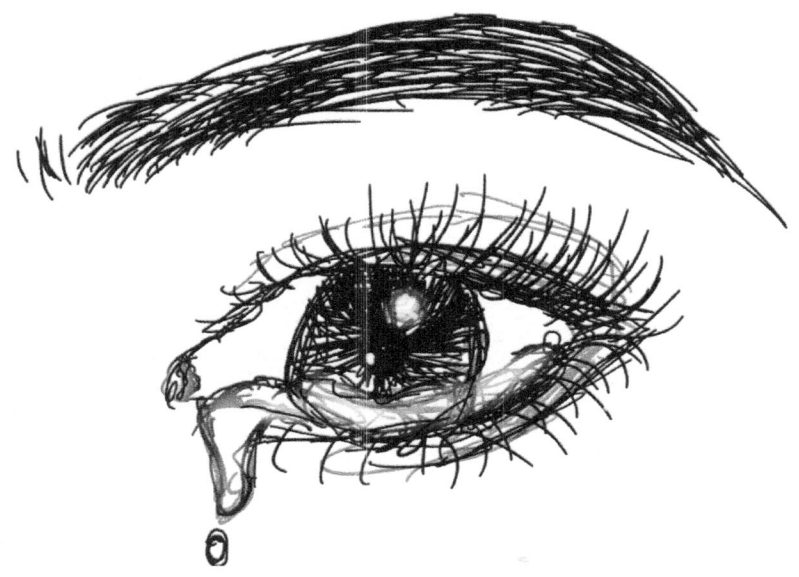

I stay busy for a reason
As to not stop
For if I stop I will think about you

TAYLOR KRISSA

Losing a friend is worse than heartbreak

Her laugh lit up the room
She could tell jokes for days
She had friends but none of them cared to stay
They all just told her it was fake

We are taught to swallow our thoughts
They are rude and interrupting and unimportant
Who asked you to speak?
Shut up and sit down
The men are saying something important

You told me to cover up
I'm showing to much skin
I didn't know loving my body was a sin

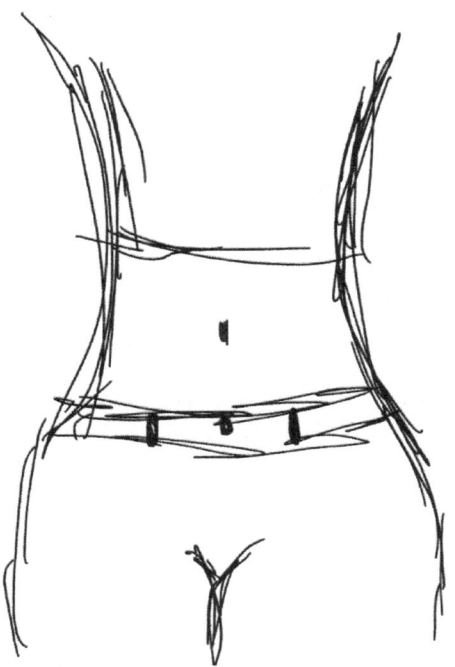

My yelling is a whisper when it's the men that are listening

He said he liked me all natural
How do I tell him he hasn't even seen me without makeup

You have a perfect guy trying to hand you all his love
But the baggage in your past occupies all the space you have.

Your mind is like a puzzle I need to solve
Your heart is a broken bottle
But your love is is like a safe I don't have the key to

YOU'RE NOT TOO YOUNG TO HAVE SORROW

JUST BECAUSE IM YOUNG

I don't want to sleep yet.
Because then I must wake up in the morning
I don't want to start tomorrow yet
Let me live this freedom I have alone tonight.
Before all the responsibilities come

Is it bad that I miss being sad?

I cant cry anymore. Im so sad but I cant cry. I need to breakdown. I miss having feelings. I feel like im just going through the motions. I'm just numb. At least when I was sad I had a personality. What am I now? Im alive but I'm not living

My mom doesn't understand that she lost her happy little girl a long time ago

You don't know what im feeling
These thoughts in my head are piling up but I won't let them explode
No I must keep my cool
No one must know you are breaking
You must be perfect
You cannot let them see you cry
Stop being dramatic
Do not let them think you are weak
Keep your stupid thoughts to yourself
For it will only hurt you if you say them aloud
Because that's when they become real

I hate that anyone only sees me as the dumb energetic friend. I have so many ideas and thoughts and want to have so many conversations. No one thinks of me like that though. So I will remain stupid with a pretty smile.

If my pillow could could hear
I bet it would tell me it isn't worth the tears
It would say "Go to sleep, tomorrow is another day"
"Rest for now, happiness isn't that far away."

I feel like I am a sink overflowing

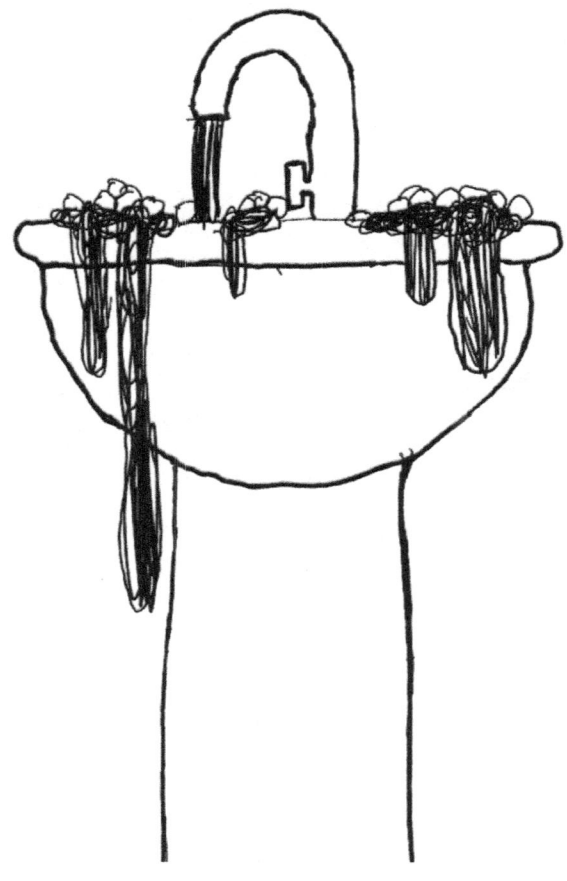

I wish I could go back
Restart my life with all the knowledge I currently have
I don think I've ever made a good decision
Im behind on everything
I can't catch up
Everything has gone wrong and nothing I do can stop it
Who was gonna tell me life is this hard?

TAYLOR KRISSA

I wish I could change my body to look like the models.

Why would anybody want her
Her waste is too wide
Her breast are too small
Her smile is too dull
Her lips are too thin
Her nose is crooked
Her hair was a mess
She wasn't pretty
She was out of order
As I looked in the mirror I was her

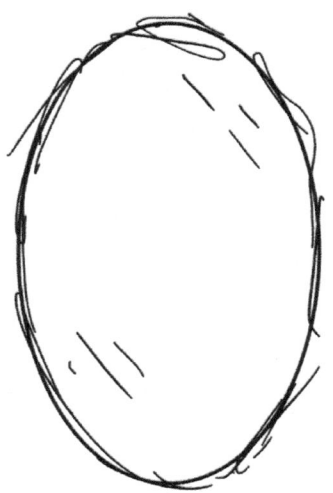

They asked what happened to me
God I wish I knew.

And in that moment, the pain you gave me disappeared, just like the love we shared, and yet, I could never forget the memories we made together

People say the best part of their day is laying down and going to sleep
But how can that be
As I lay down my mind works the most
The overthinking happens
The tears come flooding out of my eyes
This is why I say I'm tired

I have so many options
But no choices

TAYLOR KRISSA

I am too young to feel what I'm feeling

I wish I was only tired physically

I am fighting for my life under these arms that are pining me down

I was too scared to yell for help
I didn't want to cause a scene

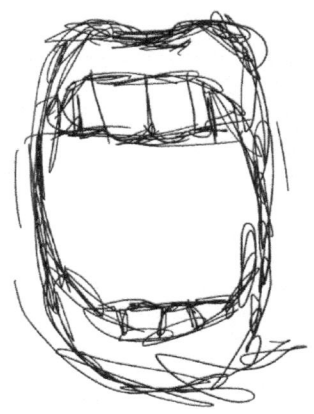

Ive heard stories of how when someones heart breaks so does a piece of our world.
That's how the Grand Canyon was formed
The story of young girl with her heart broken
Her mothers death made her split the earth clean open

She was my rock
She was my world
I never knew how much I loved her
Until she was really gone.
She is all I think about
She is the only person I want to see as I grow up
hold her close while you have her

Her smile meant the the world
Her laugh filled the room
Now the room is empty
And the world means nothing
Everyone loved her for her
Everyone misses her for her

JUST BECAUSE IM YOUNG

Fathers are supposed to help their daughters
Not break their heart
How can you step on my neck while yelling at me to get up?

Who is supposed to teach me how braid my hair
What am I supposed to do when I get my period
What if my friends talk about me at school
How do I paint my nails
Mommy how do I know he is the one
Do you like him
Mommy which shirt looks better?
How do I know what bra to buy
Mom can you teach me how to do this
Mom I need to talk about my feelings
Mommy I miss you
     - all daughters deserve a mother

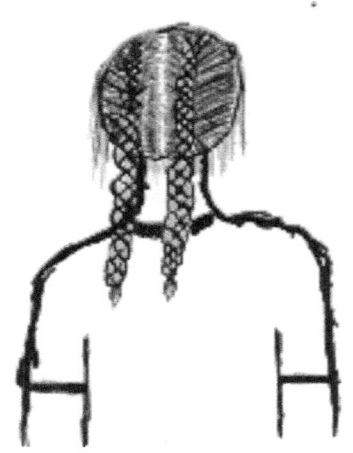

I hate going to my friends houses
I'd meet their parents and think it was weird that they're still together.
You guys are lucky that doesn't usually happen.
Why can't my parents still be together?
How did you guys make it work?
Tell me your secrets so I can whisper them to my mother,
So she can stop crying on the bathroom floor.
Tell me what I can do so that I can see my father more than just on the weekends.
I didn't like having two christmas' or two birthdays
Or having to pack a bag every Friday
How did you love each other so long?
How do you still make each other laugh?
When all I get is my family splitting in half

Its like I am watching you fade away
Please try harder
Get your life together
God you are so lazy
I don't want you to end up in the streets
Think about your future
Not all is lost
Please try
If not for you then for me

YOU'RE NOT TOO YOUNG TO FALL IN LOVE

TAYLOR KRISSA

I still get butterflies when I hear your name

She is so bored
Bored of school, friends, family, speaking, breathing, living
But he was like the funniest joke in the world
Like the prettiest sunset
The loveliest song
He was like a breath of fresh air while she was drowning in thoughts

Kiss me until I'm split open and shoved with sunshine
Until I fall to the fall and shatter into a million pieces
Kiss me until I cry or die or until I finally feel alive inside
Kiss me, you're the only thing in the world
Kiss me, I love you
Kiss me until I know what love is
Kiss me toxic
Kiss me until it's too much, till I'm buried six feet under, kiss me until I'm sick
Kiss me until I don't want too anymore
Kiss me kiss me kiss me kiss me
Kiss me because I need to
Kiss me till the sun stops shining. Until there's no more water on earth. Kiss me until everyone stops breathing and it's just you
Kiss me until it's only you ever
Kiss me until I'm blind
Until I can only see you. So, my ears only listen for your voice.
Kiss me until I fall until I shatter
Kiss me until I feel alive

Its not about about the brown curly hair and bright blue eyes
Its about holding the door and kisses goodnight
Its your thoughtful communication
And your hand fitting in mine

Your body and your face
They may be nice
but the way you say my name is
What gives me butterflies

It's your skin touching mine
And the passion between our kiss
The warmth of your breath
And the taste of your lips

Every shooting star.
Every birthday wish
Every dandelion,
Every 11:11
Every wishbone
Every wishing well
Is spent on you

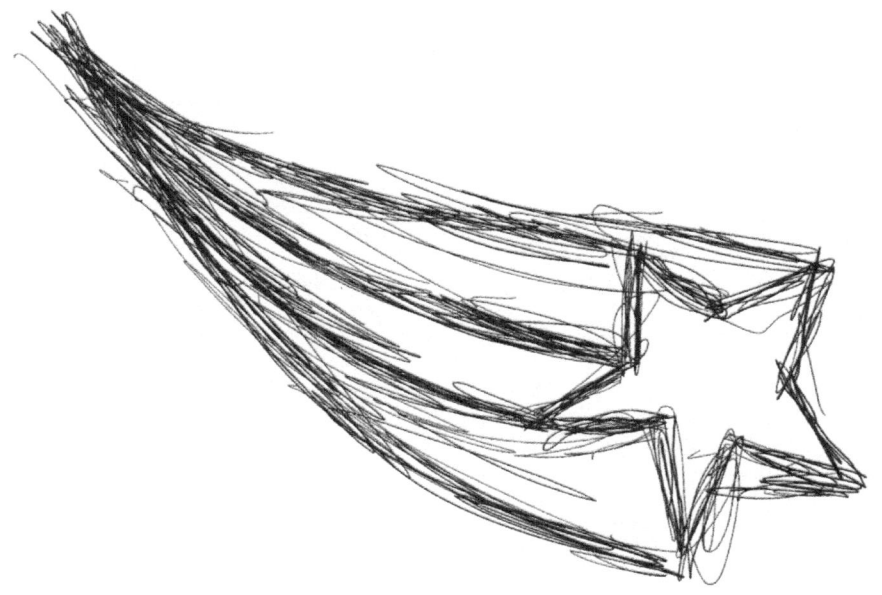

TAYLOR KRISSA

Who needs drugs when I have you

You were so easy to fall in love with

Let's run away
I don't care where
As long as I'm with you I know I'm not scared

Your dad thought you wrong
You don't use me as your shield
We protect each other with our word and our love

TAYLOR KRISSA

When I'm away from you I feel like a burnt out bulb
When I'm with you I feel as bright as a diamond
This is why I never want to say goodbye

I have a special version of myself for everyone
Personalities molded around different types of people
Little did you know
I never made a version of myself for you
That was the real me

TAYLOR KRISSA

The silence was so comforting with you

You were my sun in the cold winter
   -apricity

And in that moment, they realized they were in love with them. They realized the only person they wanted, was the person they couldn't have. They We're heartbroken, yet relieved. They were relived because they're still friends, but heartbroken because that's all they'll ever be. Or at least, that's what they thought

Every love story started somewhere
Some are poems
Some are books
Some are series

YOU'RE NOT TOO YOUNG TO FEEL TRUE HAPPINESS

I love when people dance like there is no one watching
I love Burning a new candle
Laughing so hard that my stomach hurts
I love the feeling of falling in love
I love the smell of rain and
Flustered eye contact
I love the feeling of achievement and
Road trips
I love writing the perfect poem

You do not see how beautiful you look
How your eyes light up at sunsets. Puppies, or the smell of chocolates
You do not see how effortlessly gorgeous you look when you think no one is watching
You do not notice how everyone smiles when your laugh fills the room
So the next time someone tells you how beautiful you are, believe them

She breathed in the air around her
Took in the colors and motions of the flowers
The mountains and valleys around her
Completely alone in that field
But the only time she has truly ever felt happy

TAYLOR KRISSA

When they leave you will think that is the end
You are so young
You will find someone again

This is me
I don't have the perfect body nor the perfect smile
I have the perfect heart which will someday match with someone else

How do i know if this is a new beginning or the start of another chapter?

Fall in love when your ready not when your lonely

To all the young girls who relate to these peoms, thank you. Writing this we wanted to make something that you guys could relate to. If your not comfortable talking to anyone, sit down and read a couple of these poems, and know you're not alone.

ABOUT THE AUTHOR

Emily Michniak And Taylor Krissa

Emily Michniak is a 17-year old highschool student. Taylor Krissa is a 16-year old high schooler. They wrote, illustrated, and self-published their very first book,"just becuase im young." Which explores love, grief, depression,and happiness.

Made in the USA
Monee, IL
25 January 2023

26278080R00069